© 2002 by Barbour Publishing, Inc.

ISBN 1-58660-437-6

Cover art © Stockbyte.com

Poem by Wanda Royer on pages 26 and 27 © 2002. Used by permission.

Published by Barbour Books, an imprint of Barbour Publishing, Inc.,
P.O. Box 719, Uhrichsville, Ohio 44683
www.barbourbooks.com

 Member of the
Evangelical Christian
Publishers Association

Printed in China.

WISHING YOU A HAPPY BIRTHDAY!

Rebecca Germany

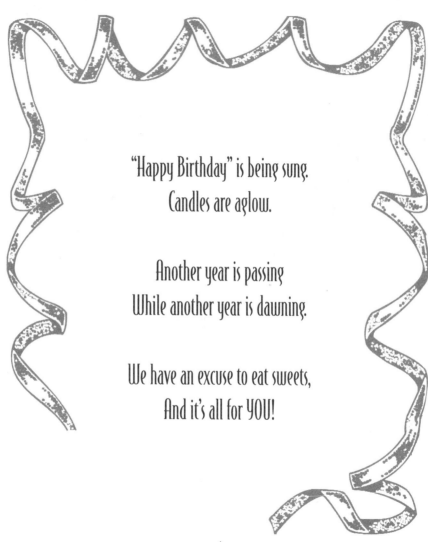

"Happy Birthday" is being sung.
Candles are aglow.

Another year is passing
While another year is dawning.

We have an excuse to eat sweets,
And it's all for YOU!

4

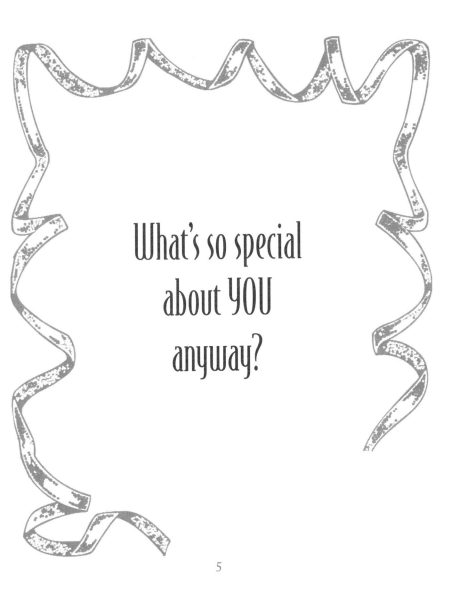

What's so special
about YOU
anyway?

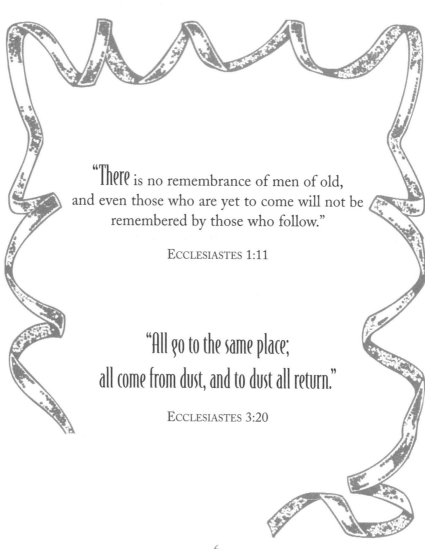

"There is no remembrance of men of old,
and even those who are yet to come will not be
remembered by those who follow."

ECCLESIASTES 1:11

"All go to the same place;
all come from dust, and to dust all return."

ECCLESIASTES 3:20

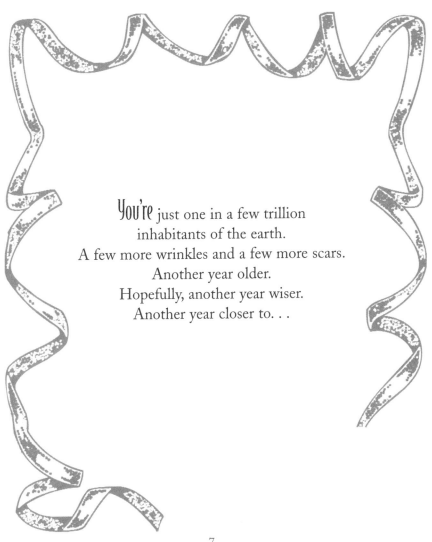

You're just one in a few trillion
inhabitants of the earth.
A few more wrinkles and a few more scars.
Another year older.
Hopefully, another year wiser.
Another year closer to. . .

STOP

I won't let you lament any more,

because...

You are
SOMEONE
very special to...

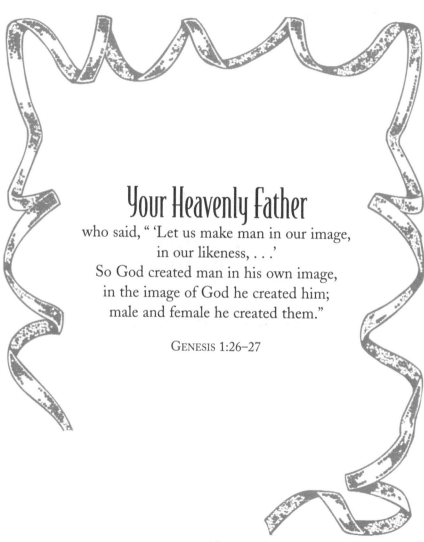

Your Heavenly Father

who said, " 'Let us make man in our image,
in our likeness, . . .'
So God created man in his own image,
in the image of God he created him;
male and female he created them."

GENESIS 1:26–27

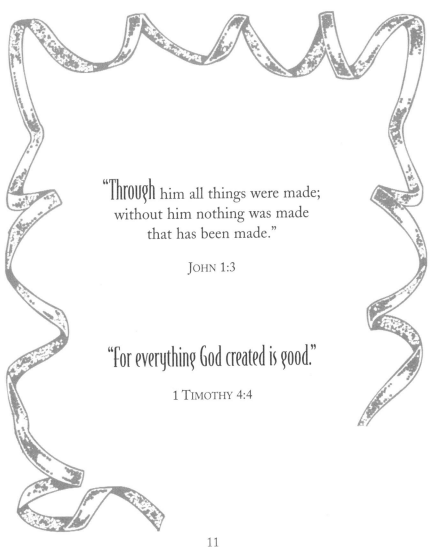

"Through him all things were made;
without him nothing was made
that has been made."

JOHN 1:3

"For everything God created is good."

1 TIMOTHY 4:4

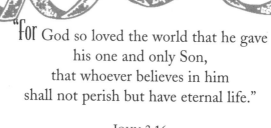

"For God so loved the world that he gave
his one and only Son,
that whoever believes in him
shall not perish but have eternal life."

JOHN 3:16

"But God demonstrates his own love for us in this:
While we were still sinners, Christ died for us."

ROMANS 5:8

"If you, then, though you are evil,
know how to give good gifts to your children,
how much more will your Father in heaven
give good gifts to those who ask him!"

MATTHEW 7:11

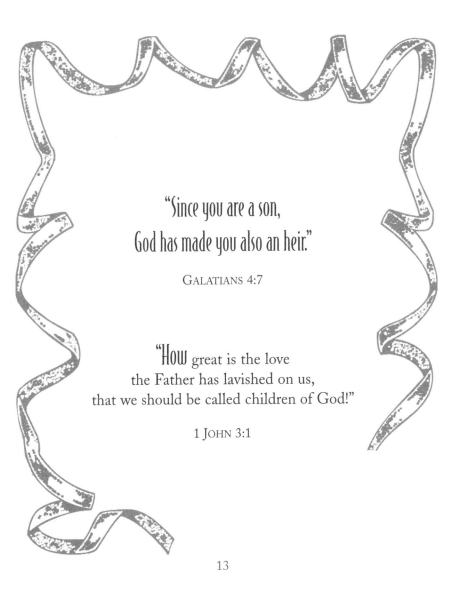

"Since you are a son,
God has made you also an heir."

GALATIANS 4:7

"How great is the love
the Father has lavished on us,
that we should be called children of God!"

1 JOHN 3:1

13

Your Birthday

Defined as the day you entered into the world where larger people could cuddle you and coo over you, pinch your round cheeks and officially welcome you to the family. It was the day you took your first move toward independence. It was the first day when you could make your voice heard and breathe a breath of air.

But even before that "birthday" you were someone very special who was being watched over and cared for. Every aspect of you was knit together by a master weaver. He knew what your body would look like. He knew the kind of personality that would propel your actions through all the days of your life.

14

Even after your day of birth He watched over your every move, knowing when you sat and when you rose, when you were busy and when you rested. He waited patiently for you to grow in knowledge of Him and held His breath in anticipation of the day you would acknowledge His hand on your life.

Though many of your birthdays have been celebrated, He still longs to be the first one you turn to for anything. He knows you best, because He was there with you from the start and laid the foundation of who you are.

Never fail to start each new day of life acknowledging this awesome craftsman. He has never made a mistake, and none of His works have ever malfunctioned.

READ PSALM 139

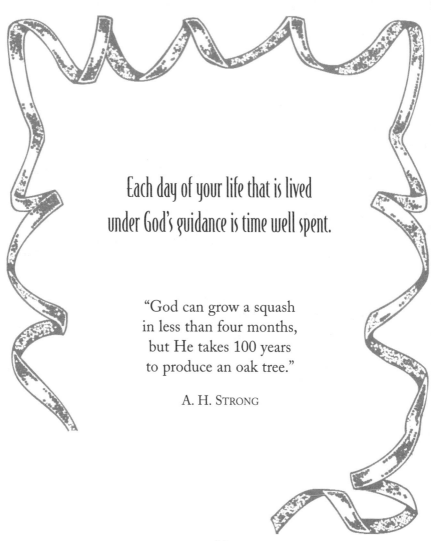

Each day of your life that is lived
under God's guidance is time well spent.

"God can grow a squash
in less than four months,
but He takes 100 years
to produce an oak tree."

A. H. STRONG

"Every experience God gives us,
every person He puts in our lives,
is the perfect preparation for the future
that only He can see."

CORRIE TEN BOOM

"And we know that in all things
God works for the good of those who love him,
who have been called according to his purpose."

ROMANS 8:28

"'For I know the plans I have for you,'
declares the LORD,
'plans to prosper you and not to harm you,
plans to give you hope and a future.'"

JEREMIAH 29:11

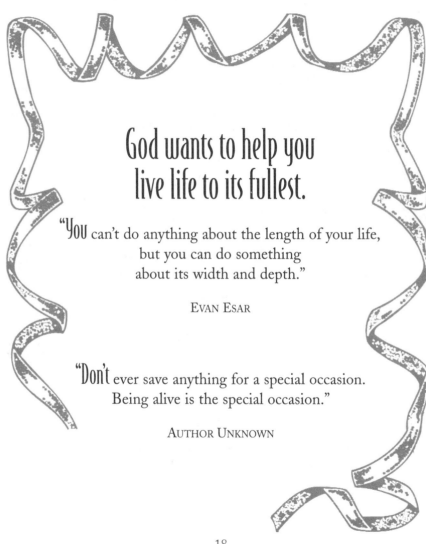

God wants to help you live life to its fullest.

"You can't do anything about the length of your life,
but you can do something
about its width and depth."

EVAN ESAR

"Don't ever save anything for a special occasion.
Being alive is the special occasion."

AUTHOR UNKNOWN

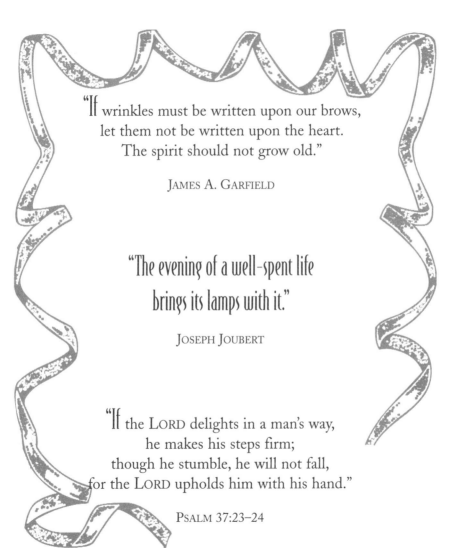

"If wrinkles must be written upon our brows,
let them not be written upon the heart.
The spirit should not grow old."

JAMES A. GARFIELD

"The evening of a well-spent life
brings its lamps with it."

JOSEPH JOUBERT

"If the LORD delights in a man's way,
he makes his steps firm;
though he stumble, he will not fall,
for the LORD upholds him with his hand."

PSALM 37:23–24

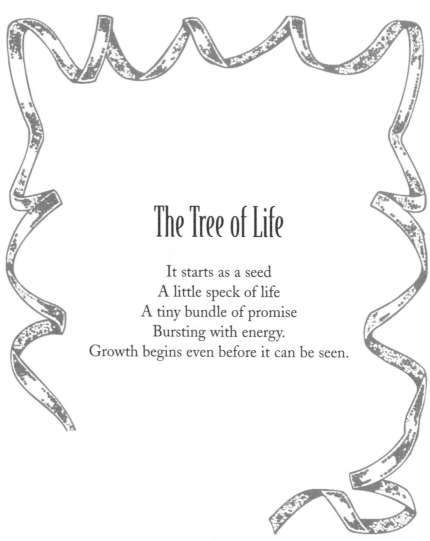

The Tree of Life

It starts as a seed
A little speck of life
A tiny bundle of promise
Bursting with energy.
Growth begins even before it can be seen.

Soon there is a sprout, tiny and fragile,
but visible to all.
It will need some protection and nurture.
Still growth is rapid.
The sapling is flexible in the wind and eager to
branch out in all directions.
It reaches toward the sky,
not limited by any ceiling.

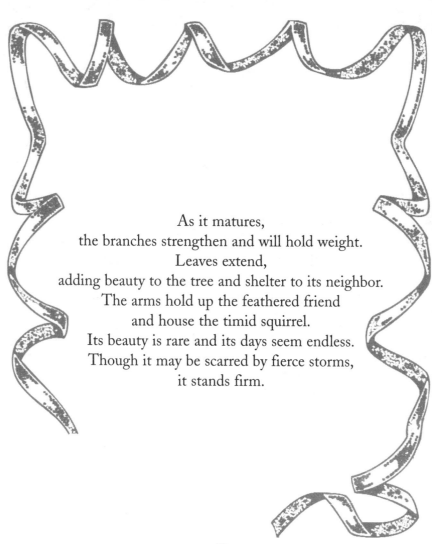

As it matures,
the branches strengthen and will hold weight.
Leaves extend,
adding beauty to the tree and shelter to its neighbor.
The arms hold up the feathered friend
and house the timid squirrel.
Its beauty is rare and its days seem endless.
Though it may be scarred by fierce storms,
it stands firm.

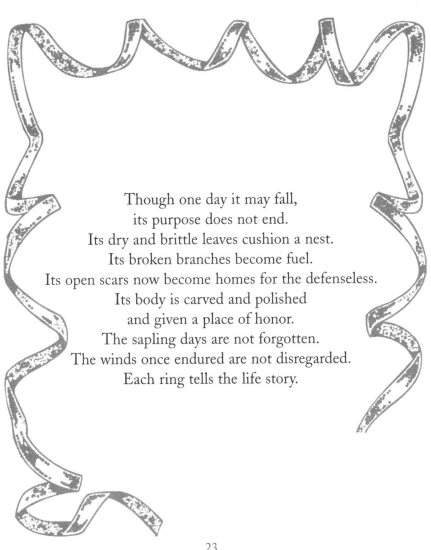

Though one day it may fall,
its purpose does not end.
Its dry and brittle leaves cushion a nest.
Its broken branches become fuel.
Its open scars now become homes for the defenseless.
Its body is carved and polished
and given a place of honor.
The sapling days are not forgotten.
The winds once endured are not disregarded.
Each ring tells the life story.

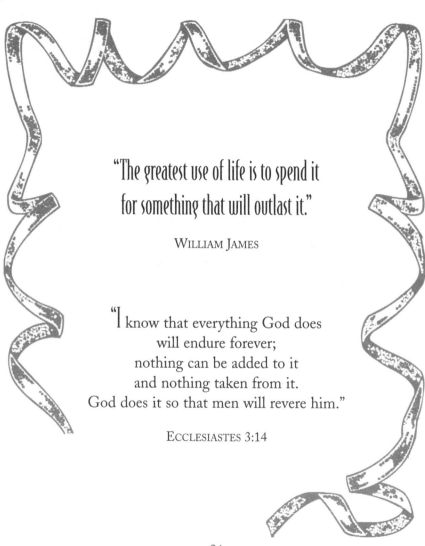

"The greatest use of life is to spend it
for something that will outlast it."

WILLIAM JAMES

"I know that everything God does
will endure forever;
nothing can be added to it
and nothing taken from it.
God does it so that men will revere him."

ECCLESIASTES 3:14

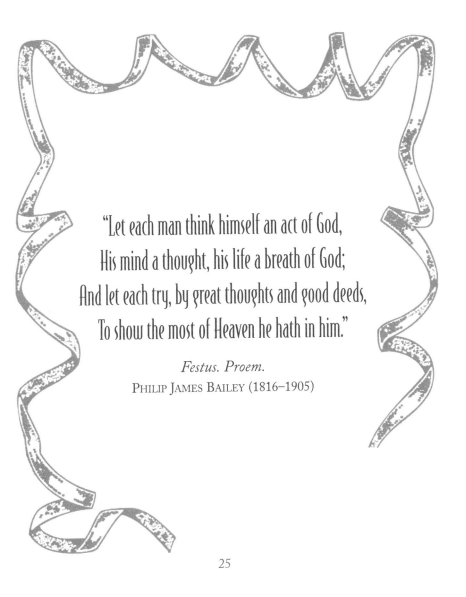

"Let each man think himself an act of God,
His mind a thought, his life a breath of God;
And let each try, by great thoughts and good deeds,
To show the most of Heaven he hath in him."

Festus. Proem.
PHILIP JAMES BAILEY (1816–1905)

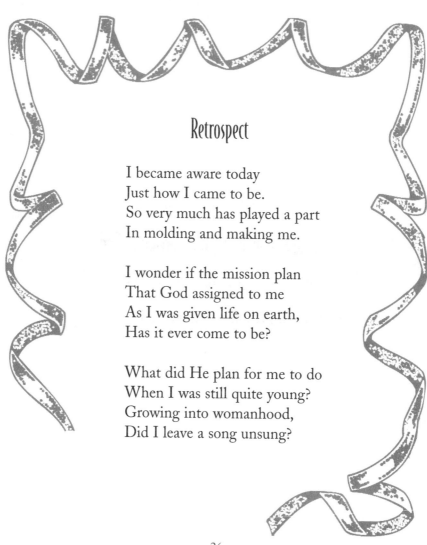

Retrospect

I became aware today
Just how I came to be.
So very much has played a part
In molding and making me.

I wonder if the mission plan
That God assigned to me
As I was given life on earth,
Has it ever come to be?

What did He plan for me to do
When I was still quite young?
Growing into womanhood,
Did I leave a song unsung?

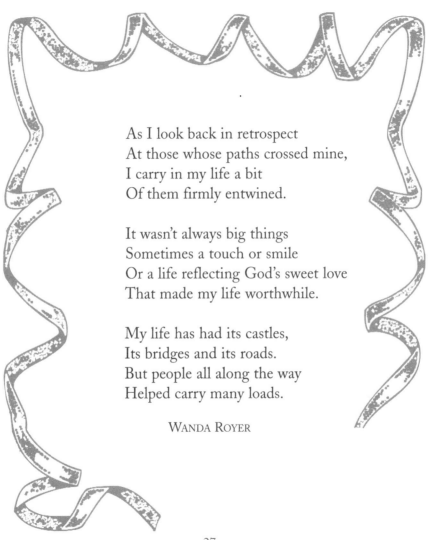

As I look back in retrospect
At those whose paths crossed mine,
I carry in my life a bit
Of them firmly entwined.

It wasn't always big things
Sometimes a touch or smile
Or a life reflecting God's sweet love
That made my life worthwhile.

My life has had its castles,
Its bridges and its roads.
But people all along the way
Helped carry many loads.

WANDA ROYER

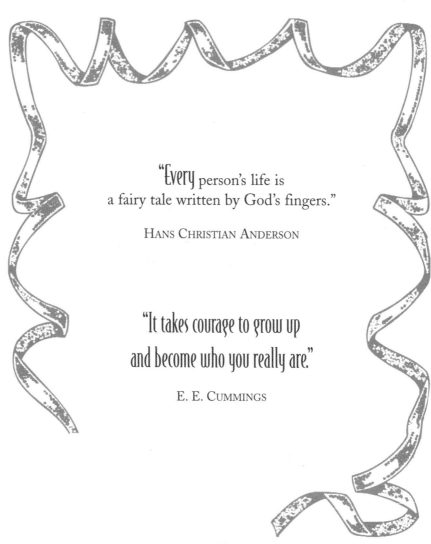

"Every person's life is
a fairy tale written by God's fingers."

Hans Christian Anderson

"It takes courage to grow up
and become who you really are."

E. E. Cummings

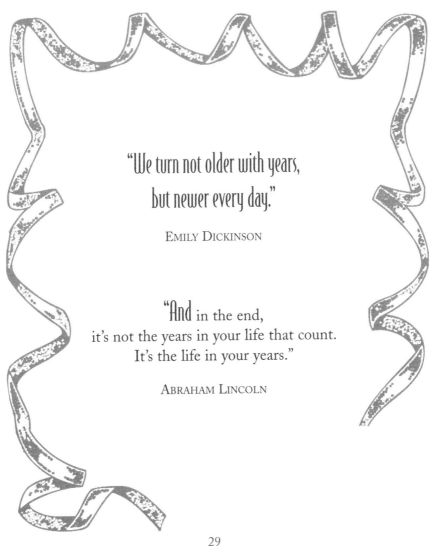

"We turn not older with years,
but newer every day."

EMILY DICKINSON

"And in the end,
it's not the years in your life that count.
It's the life in your years."

ABRAHAM LINCOLN

You are also someone
very special to...
ME!

"I thank my God every time I remember you."

PHILIPPIANS 1:3

"It is one mark of a friend that
he makes you wish to be at your best
while you are with him."

HENRY VAN DYKE

And I have a very special
birthday WISH for you.

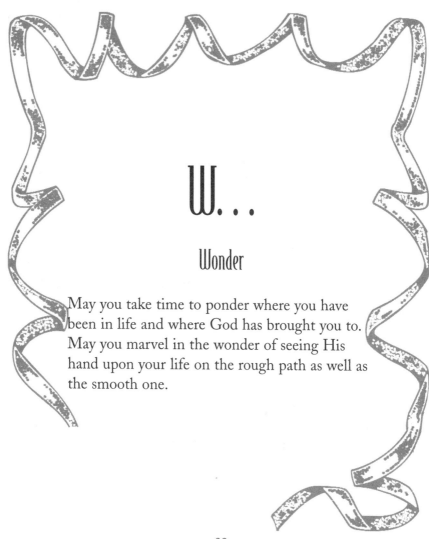

W...

Wonder

May you take time to ponder where you have been in life and where God has brought you to. May you marvel in the wonder of seeing His hand upon your life on the rough path as well as the smooth one.

"**Imagine** yourself as a living house. God comes in to rebuild that house. At first, perhaps, you can understand what He is doing. He is getting the drains right and stopping the leaks in the roof and so on: you knew that those jobs needed doing and so you are not surprised. But presently, He starts knocking the house about in a way that hurts abominably and does not seem to make sense. What on earth is He up to? The explanation is that He is building quite a different house from the one you thought of, throwing out a new wing here, putting on an extra floor there, running up towers, making courtyards. You thought you were going to be made into a decent little cottage: but He is building a palace."

C. S. Lewis

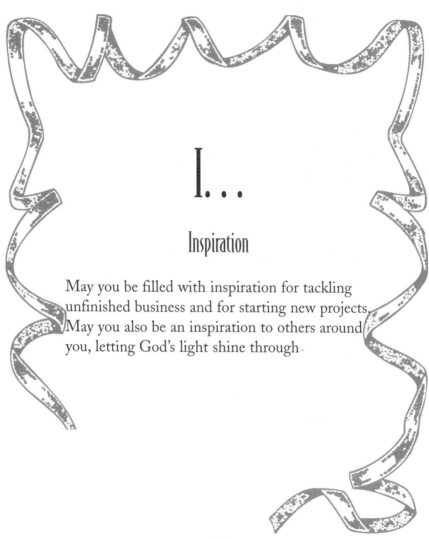

I...

Inspiration

May you be filled with inspiration for tackling unfinished business and for starting new projects. May you also be an inspiration to others around you, letting God's light shine through.

34

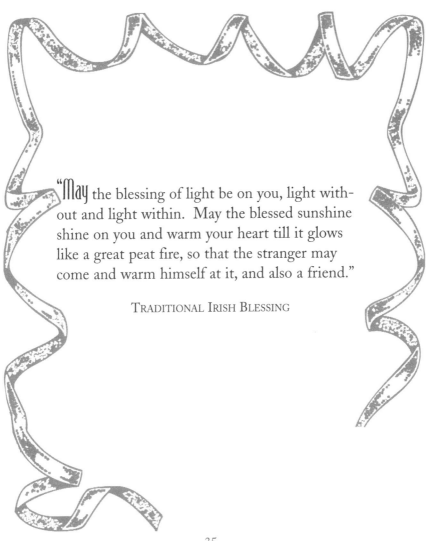

"May the blessing of light be on you, light without and light within. May the blessed sunshine shine on you and warm your heart till it glows like a great peat fire, so that the stranger may come and warm himself at it, and also a friend."

TRADITIONAL IRISH BLESSING

S...

Sadness and Silliness

May your days be filled with a healthy balance of
sadness and silliness. We all need those sad times
to slow us down—time to reflect, time to bow
humbly at the Lord's feet and seek His loving
guidance. We also need those silly times that
remind us of the sheer joy of living this life God
gave us.

"The best and most beautiful things in the world
cannot be seen or even touched.
They must be felt with the heart."

HELEN KELLER

"There is a time for everything,
and a season for every activity under heaven....
a time to weep and a time to laugh,
a time to mourn and a time to dance."

ECCLESIASTES 3:1, 4

37

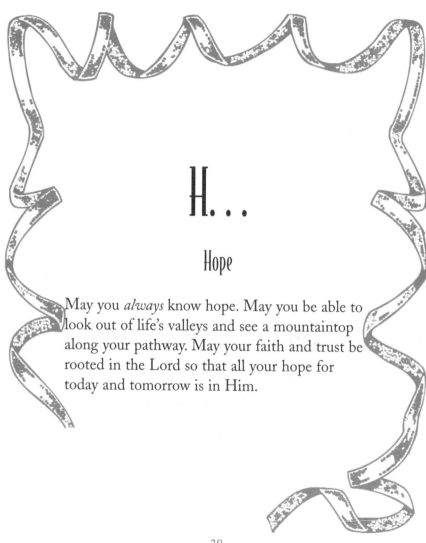

H...

Hope

May you *always* know hope. May you be able to look out of life's valleys and see a mountaintop along your pathway. May your faith and trust be rooted in the Lord so that all your hope for today and tomorrow is in Him.

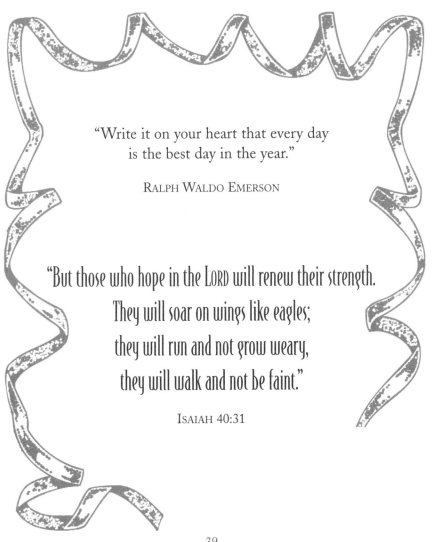

"Write it on your heart that every day
is the best day in the year."

RALPH WALDO EMERSON

"But those who hope in the LORD will renew their strength.
They will soar on wings like eagles;
they will run and not grow weary,
they will walk and not be faint."

ISAIAH 40:31

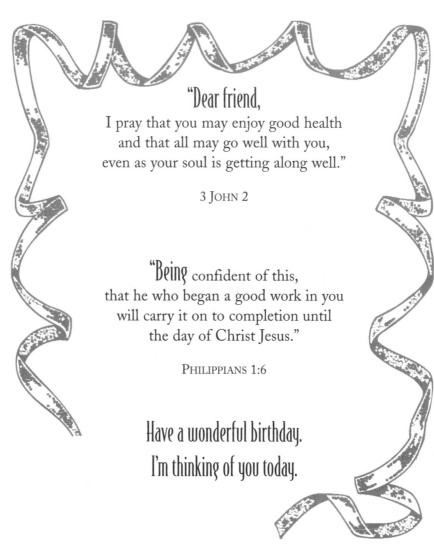

"Dear friend,
I pray that you may enjoy good health
and that all may go well with you,
even as your soul is getting along well."

3 JOHN 2

"Being confident of this,
that he who began a good work in you
will carry it on to completion until
the day of Christ Jesus."

PHILIPPIANS 1:6

Have a wonderful birthday.
I'm thinking of you today.